MAKE YOUR OWN
Celebrity
SCRAPBOOK

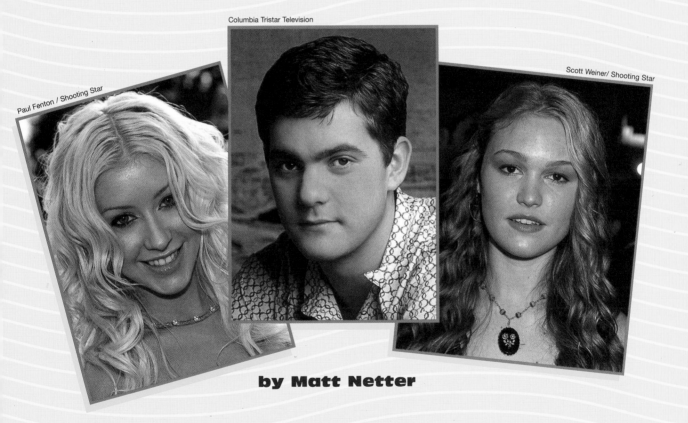

Columbia Tristar Television

Paul Fenton / Shooting Star

Scott Weiner/ Shooting Star

by Matt Netter

Add Your Own Favorite Photos to the Scrapbook Pages!

Reader's Digest
Children's Books™

Pleasantville, New York • Montréal, Québec

making MUSIC

Pop goes the world! The new millennium brought with it a pop-music explosion. For the past few years, the charts have been ruled by boy bands, teen queens, and other young pop rockers. Back in 1997, groups such as Hanson and the Spice Girls opened the door for young stars like Britney Spears, Christina Aguilera, 'N Sync, and the Backstreet Boys. The music scene hasn't been the same since.

Boy Band Fever

'N Sync and the Backstreet Boys have more in common than just being pop vocal groups from Orlando, Florida. Both groups, despite their millions of fans, were written off as gimmick acts by critics early on in their careers. These pop chart mainstays have certainly proved the skeptics wrong. They've broken all kinds of industry sales records; the two groups have had seven multi-platinum (multi-million selling) records between them, and they sell out concert arenas all over the world. Both 'N Sync and the Backstreet Boys are determined to take their careers to the next level. They've learned to write songs, play instruments, and experiment with new sounds and styles. As a result, they've been steadily attracting fans of all ages, not just teens. If this trend continues, the sky's the limit for these heartthrobs.

'N Sync

Backstreet Boys

Did you know...

Nick Carter and Brian Littrell are such inseparable friends that, among family and friends, they are known as Frick and Frack.

Teen Queens Rule

When Britney Spears first came on the scene, critics compared her to an '80s teen star, calling her "the Debbie Gibson for a new generation." Now, with three multi-platinum CDs, several sold-out world tours, and all kinds of awards under her belt, she's being hailed as the Madonna for the new millennium. Her first CD, *Baby...One More Time*, sold millions as did the follow-up, *Oops, I Did It Again*. This singing and dancing diva has it all—glamour, energy, and talent.

Blonde and beautiful Christina Aguilera hasn't been far behind. A New York native, Christina started her career at age eight when she appeared on TV's *Star Search*. With a powerful voice, loads of ambition, attitude to spare, and smash hits like "Genie In A Bottle," "What A Girl Wants," and "Come On Over," Christina has turned the music world on its ear.

Britney and Christina aren't the only female singers in the spotlight. Jessica Simpson, who was trained as a gospel singer, won acclaim for her extraordinary voice when she branched out into a livelier pop sound. Multi-talented Mandy Moore not only makes hit records, but has also starred in her own TV show on MTV and has her first movie in the works.

Destiny's Child

Destiny Calls

The rise of boy bands has been matched by a wave of exciting new R&B (rhythm & blues) girl groups that feature high-energy music and hot fashions. Texas trio Destiny's Child—Kelly Rowland, Beyoncé Knowles, and Michelle Williams—are one of the most exciting acts in music today. The group's incredible combination of talent, attitude, beauty, and style has produced a string of number-one hits including "Say My Name," "Bills, Bills, Bills," and "Independent Woman, Part I." On stage, the girls are electrifying, with daring outfits and stunning choreography. Destiny's Child has been showered with all kinds of awards, including Grammys, Billboard Music Awards, MTV Video Music Awards, and more. Gorgeous, charismatic, and talented, Destiny's Child is destined to be around for a long time.

Christina

Did you know...

When they were younger, both Britney Spears and Christina Aguilera were members of the cast of *The Mickey Mouse Club* TV show.

SINGING sensations

Put your photo faves
on these pages.

If I could choose two singers
to sing a duet, they would be

_____

_____

My favorite singers are

_____

_____

_____

_____

_____

Girl Talk
Ever wonder how singers unwind after a big concert? Both Britney Spears and Christina Aguilera have said they take bubble baths.

great GROUPS

My favorite bands are

and shining STARS

Fast Fact

Boy bands are not just an American phenomenon. In Europe, boy bands rule the radio. Five, Westlife, and BBMak are among the most popular.

My favorite songs by a group are

_____
_____
_____
_____
_____

HIT-MAKERS and

The music star whose autograph
I would most love to have is

_____

_____

_____

Oh, Brother!

When Aaron Carter came on the scene, Backstreet Boys fans only knew him as Nick Carter's little brother. Then he toured as an opening act for BSB. Now he's a full-fledged star in his own right.

HEARTTHROBS

If I could sing a duet
with any performer, I would pick

who's NUMBER ONE?

If I wrote a song, the title would be

_____

_____

_____

If I were stranded on a desert island and could bring three CDs, they would be

_____

_____

_____

MOVIE madness

The teen boom in music has been matched by a flood of teen movies, the likes of which haven't been seen since the '80s when movies like *The Breakfast Club* and *Sixteen Candles* lit up the screen. Thanks to a slew of recent romantic comedies, horror movies, and outrageous spoofs, a new wave of movie stars has captured moviegoers' attention and their affections.

Katie

Columbia Tristar Television

Leading Ladies

There's certainly no shortage of beautiful young women on the big screen (Tara Reid, James King, and Jennifer Love Hewitt, to name just a few). But what's striking about today's teenage and twenty-something actresses is that so many possess the acting potential to be future Academy Award winners. *Dawson's Creek* star Katie Holmes (*Wonder Boys, Phone Booth, Abandon*) has proven she can tackle just about any role given to her. Julia Stiles, who made her acclaimed debut in the TV mini-series *The '60s*, has played a wide variety of roles (*Save the Last Dance, State and Main, The Bourne Identity*) that showcase her talent. Rachael Leigh Cook has been dubbed this generation's Winona Ryder, and with good reason. She can be adorable (*Josie and the Pussycats*), charming (*She's All That*), haunting (*The Eighteenth Angel*), and dramatic (*Tangled*). Another versatile young actress is Kirsten Dunst. She can act sophisticated (*All Forgotten*), devious (*Virgin Suicides*), or lovable (*Drop Dead Gorgeous, Spider-Man*).

Gorgeous Guys

In the old days, they called them matinee idols—handsome young actors whose presence on screen guaranteed a hit at the box office. Today, Hollywood calls them hotties. At the top of the list are Chris Klein, Freddie Prinze, Jr., Ryan Phillippe, Josh Hartnett, and Joshua Jackson. Which one you pay to see depends on your taste. If you're into the modest, boy-next-door type, Freddie Prinze, Jr. (*Summer Catch, Scooby-Doo*) is your guy. If you like emotionally deep, tenderhearted guys with wholesome good looks, then Chris Klein (*Rollerball, American Pie II*) is a dream come true. For girls who like a guy with a sense of humor, there's a double dose of Joshua Jackson, who can be found on both the small screen (*Dawson's Creek*) and the big screen (*Lone Star State of Mind*). Ryan Phillippe (*Igby Goes Down*) embodies the irresistible, brooding type, but if you just can't resist the bad boy, Josh Hartnett (*40 Days and 40 Nights*) is the one to watch.

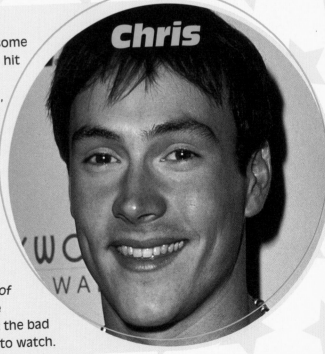

Chris

Lance

APRF/ Clavel/ Shooting Star

What Are Friends For?

falls into a category all by itself. And it's not just because the movie features Britney Spears in her first starring role, but because it's a combination musical, comedy, and adventure film. 'N Sync's Lance Bass and Joey Fatone will also be making their big screen debuts soon in the romantic comedy *On the El*. Another film worth keeping an eye out for is *Sorority Rule*. Described as an *Animal House* for girls, the comedy stars Amy Smart, Marla Sokoloff, Natasha Lyonne, Clea Duvall, Katherine Heigl, Zooey Deschanel, and Selma Blair. With a cast like that, *Sorority Rule* may be one of those movies that's looked back on as a launching pad for stardom.

Hit Flicks

In terms of movie tickets, teenagers translate to big bucks at the box office. Some of the most successful recent teen films include outrageous comedies (*American Pie I* and *II*, *Road Trip*, *Get Over It*, *Teen Movie*), TV-show-inspired hits (*Charlie's Angels*, *Josie and the Pussycats*, *Spider Man*, *Scooby-Doo*), dramas (*Tart*, *Texas Rangers*, *Here on Earth*), romantic comedies (*She's All That*, *Loser*, *Summer Catch,* and *Save the Last Dance* starring Julia Stiles) and horror flicks (*Abandon*, *13 Ghosts*, *The Forsaken*). One of the biggest hits with teens recently was *A Knight's Tale*. Fans flocked to the flick to see Australian-hottie Heath Ledger.

Julia

Scott Weiner/ Shooting Star

The hottest male actor is

Fast Fact

Titanic was the highest-grossing movie of all time. The film made over a billion dollars worldwide. Its star, Leonardo DiCaprio, now commands $20 million per movie!

The most beautiful actress is

FAVORITE films

My all-time favorite movies
that I could watch a million times are

and shining STARS

Fast Fact

Chris Klein's breakout role was in 1999's *Election*, with Matthew Broderick and Reese Witherspoon.

The movies that made me laugh the most were

_____

_____

_____

hollywood's HOTTEST!

If they made a movie of my life,
it would be called

_____

_____

Notable and Quotable

"Everywhere you turn, you see me in a movie, and I'm sorry. At this point, people must be saying, 'Biggs again? Can't we get away from this guy?'"
—Jason Biggs

The star that would play me would be

_____

_____

The best-dressed
male and female movie stars are

_____

_____

The worst-dressed male and female movie stars are

_____

_____

TV time

There have never been more TV shows aimed at teenagers than there are today. These days, kids can channel surf all day long and be entertained by a legion of emerging teen actors.

Frankie

Cool Comedies

Many of the funniest shows on television today are teen comedies. The most outrageous comedy of all is *Malcolm in the Middle*. At the center of a comically dysfunctional family lies Malcolm (Frankie Muniz), a child genius who just wants to be a normal kid. It isn't easy with three reckless brothers and a totally fearless mom. FOX's *That '70s Show* combines a cool cast, witty story lines, and funky fashion into a hit series about six 1970s teens from Milwaukee. On *Sabrina the Teenage Witch*, Melissa Joan Hart continues to grow up in front of her audience. Hart has gone from child star, to teen star, to a TV and movie star who produces and even directs some of her own episodes.

Teen Dramas

If drama's your thing, prime-time television offers up all the romance, intrigue, jealousy, and teen trouble you can handle. *Dawson's Creek* is an ensemble drama noted for its portrayal of teen relationships. Acclaimed stars Katie Holmes, James Van Der Beek, Joshua Jackson, Michelle Williams, and Kerr Smith have each gone on to star in movies as well. *7th Heaven*, one of TV's most popular and long-running family dramas, centers around a family with everything going for it. Dad's a minister, mom's a sweetheart, and the family lives in a beautiful house with a cute dog. But the kids—Matt (Barry Watson), Mary (Jessica Biel), Lucy (Beverley Mitchell), Simon (David Gallagher), and Ruthie (Mackenzie Rosman)—just can't seem to stay out of trouble. While parents don't seem to get *Buffy the Vampire Slayer*, most teens and twenty-somethings never miss an episode. *Buffy*, which stars Sarah Michelle Gellar, is all about a bunch of teens who fight off vampires. But beneath the surface, it's really about a group of friends dealing with the problems of being a teenager.

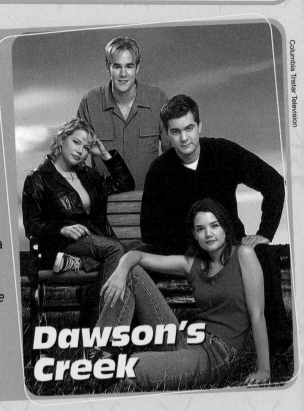

Dawson's Creek

Prime-Time Hotties

Tune into the WB, UPN, and FOX networks for more hunks and hotties than you can shake a stick at. Here's a list of TV's top guys.

☆ **Christopher Kennedy Masterson**, **Frankie Muniz**, and **Justin Berfield** of *Malcolm in the Middle*

☆ **Ashton Kutcher**, **Wilmer Valderrama**, **Danny Masterson**, and **Topher Grace** of *That '70s Show*

☆ **Joshua Jackson**, **James Van Der Beek**, and **Kerr Smith** of *Dawson's Creek*

☆ **Nicholas Brendon** and **James Marsters** of *Buffy the Vampire Slayer*

☆ **David Boreanaz** of *Angel*

☆ **Barry Watson** and **David Gallagher** of *7th Heaven*

☆ **Jason Behr**, **Colin Hanks**, and **Brendan Fehr** of *Roswell*

☆ **David Lascher** of *Sabrina the Teenage Witch*

☆ **Christopher Gorham**, **Bryce Johnson**, **Ron Lester**, **Shawn Lindsay**, and **Simon Helberg** of *Popular*

Glamour Girls

There's no shortage of talented young actresses on the TV scene either. *Dawson's Creek*'s Katie Holmes and *Buffy the Vampire Slayer*'s Sarah Michelle Gellar, in particular, are among the most in-demand actresses in Hollywood. Both stars have a knack for realism and honesty in their character portrayals. These two stars—along with *7th Heaven*'s Jessica Biel, *Sabrina the Teenage Witch*'s Melissa Joan Hart, *Dawson's Creek*'s Michelle Williams, *Buffy*'s Alyson Hannigan, *Popular*'s Leslie Bibb, and *That '70s Show*'s Mila Kunis and Laura Prepon—have crossed over quite successfully to the big screen.

Robert Sebree/ Fox

Mila

Danny Masterson: Joe Viles/ Fox; Christopher Masterson: Deborah Feingold/ Fox

My favorite TV actor is
_____
_____

screen

My favorite TV actress is

_____

_____

TV talent

My favorite comedy shows are

_____

_____

_____

The Daly News

Who's the TV host with the most—fans, that is? It's probably Carson Daly, host of MTV's *TRL*. Daly interviews the hottest pop stars and plays viewers' favorite videos.

TV Trivia

The high school where the movie *She's All That* was filmed is the same one used as Sunnydale High School in *Buffy the Vampire Slayer*.

The best TV couple is

_____

_____

CASTING a spell

If I could join the cast
of any show it would be

_____

_____

TV Trivia

The '80s hit show *Growing Pains* launched the career of Leonardo DiCaprio, who played a recurring character. Brad Pitt, Olivia d'Abo, Matthew Perry, Jennie Garth, and Hilary Swank also had guest parts on the show.

The TV character who's most like me is

_____

_____

_____

If I could be friends with any
TV character it would be

_____

from

_____

unforgettable FACES

TV Trivia

Long before he starred in movies such as *The Skulls* and *Joy Ride*, hunky Paul Walker was a TV actor. When he was 12, he had a recurring role on *Highway to Heaven* and guest starred on *Who's the Boss?*

My favorite reruns are

_____

_____

_____

MY celebrity scrapbook

Collect your favorite memorabilia (movie tickets, concert stubs, magazine clippings, autographs, etc.) and attach them to this page.

SOUVENIR page